The Carols of Christmas

Daily Advent Devotions on Classic Christmas Carols

Alan Vermilye

BROWN CHAIR BOOKS
BOOKS THAT INSPIRE

The Carols of Christmas
Daily Advent Devotions on Classic Christmas Carols

ISBN-13 Paperback: 978-1-948481-26-7
ISBN-13 Hardback: 978-1-948481-27-4

To learn more about this book and the Bible study resources that go with it, to order additional copies, or to download the answer guide, visit www.BrownChairBooks.com.

Contents

For my family, who makes every Christmas wonderful!
Merry Christmas!

Introduction

I love Christmas music—all Christmas music!

Each year, right after Thanksgiving, a switch flips in my brain, and I'm ready to crank up some Christmas tunes. Suddenly I'm transported back to Christmases past and my mom dragging out her big RCA record player from the closet to an end table in the corner of the living room. There she'd stack on a half-dozen albums, including Andy Williams, Dean Martin, Burl Ives, Bing Crosby, and, yes...*Sing Along with Mitch*, belting out in succession everything from "Silent Night" to "Rudolph the Red-Nosed Reindeer." I can still hear the crackling sound of each song through the built-in side speakers and the winding sound of the motorized arm moving out to clear the way for the next record to drop. It was wonderful!

For many of us, Christmas music holds a place in our hearts of times gone by. But Christmas carols—specifically Christian carols—can provide another very important function in that they tell the story of the nativity and explain what happened around the birth of Jesus Christ. When many of the classic carols were created, not everyone was educated and could read the Bible. These hymns were essential in spreading the gospel message and helping people learn about the good news of Jesus Christ.

Today these hymns have become so ingrained in our culture and ubiquitous with holiday celebrations that millions of people around the world joyfully sing them out, over and over again, each year. Some of the richest theological truths about the birth of our Savior are being expressed by believers and nonbelievers alike in homes, churches, stores, cars, fitness centers, the media, and more!

It's hard to find a better evangelistic outreach tool than a Christmas carol that expresses the joy, devotion, and awe-inspiring scenes of the birth of Christ. There are some who are not fans of secular musicians, who, while making no claim to Jesus, sing Christian Christmas carols. But I'm not bothered by it in the least! Think about it. God has orchestrated opportunities for unbelievers to willingly present the gospel message using the talents that He gave them. I'm good with that!

As a believer, though, what I find most interesting about some of the classic Christian carols and hymns are the stories behind them. Who wrote the hymn? What was going on in their life that perhaps inspired the hymn? And how has God used this hymn throughout time?

This was the criteria I used when choosing the four hymns found in this book. I did the best research I could, fully realizing that there are discrepancies found in the stories of hymns, which are well over one hundred years old. Then, to dig a little deeper into the biblical basis for each one, I divided them into four weeks of daily devotions for Christmas. You start each week reading the history of the carol, followed by six daily devotions. Traditionally, Advent begins on the fourth Sunday before Christmas, but the devotions found in this book are not dated and can be started anytime.

I sincerely hope you enjoy reading about the histories of these great hymns. I also pray that the heartwarming stories and inspirational verses found in the devotions bring peace and hope to you this Christmas season. Please drop me a note at www.BrownChairBooks.com. I would love to hear from you about your experience with the book.

God Bless and Merry Christmas!
Alan

"O HOLY NIGHT": A HISTORY

Y ou can almost hear the late Alex Trebek reading his cue card to contestants on the game show *Jeopardy!* "This popular Christmas hymn was written by an atheist, set to music by a Jewish composer, rejected by the church, sung on the battlefields, adopted by an American abolitionist, and the first song ever to be broadcast over airwaves to the entire world." Judges will accept either "O Holy Night" or the original French version, "Cantique de Noel."

Far more than just a trivia question though, "O Holy Night" has indelibly left its mark on history. In every Christmas Eve service for over 175 years, its inspiring lyrics and beautiful music have reduced many to tears who, except for on that one day, don't normally darken the doors of a church. Perhaps it's because the song's origin begins with that of a non-churchgoer who himself was more into wine and poetry than the singing of Christmas carols.

It all began in 1847 in the small town of Roquemaure in the south of France. The local parish priest, Father Petitjean, was excited about the renovation of their organ for Christmas Eve Mass and decided to commission a poem to celebrate the occasion. The only amateur poet in the community just happened to be an avowed atheist with vocal anti-cleric views but also a love for literature. Undeterred by what he considered a minor hindrance, Father Petitjean successfully coaxed the man, Placide Cappeau, into agreeing to his request, completely unaware of its future significance.

Growing up in Roquemaure, Cappeau was like most boys of the time: destined to follow in the family business. In this case, it was the arduous work of making wine barrels. However, his destiny was soon curtailed when, while playing one day, a friend accidentally shot Cappeau in the hand, leading to its amputation. Bearing the burden of responsibility, the friend's father paid for Cappeau's education, enabling him to attend town school and the College Roya d'Avignon, where he was a highly awarded student. Due to his handicap, Cappeau turned to a life of academia, studying literature at Nimes and law in Paris, where he acquired his law license.

However, he was soon drawn back home, where he followed in the family business in the sense that he became a local wine merchant. Cappeau, though, had many other interests, including anti-slavery activism and, for a time, mayor of the town, but his true passion was always literature. It was this passion that motivated him to agree to the priest's request, which he took very seriously.

Shortly thereafter, Cappeau was on a business trip to Paris, traveling down dusty roads in a bumpy coach. He began to imagine the difficult and dangerous journey Mary and Joseph undertook to Bethlehem that culminated in the birth of Jesus on one special night. By the time he arrived in Paris, he had written a powerful poem that he titled "Minuit, Chretiens" or "Midnight, Christians." Later, the work became more widely known as "Cantique de Noel" or "Christmas Song." Inspired by his own work, Cappeau reached out to a friend—a French composer, teacher, and music critic—to set his words to music.

Adolphe Charles Adams was well qualified for the task requested of him. The son of a well-known classical musician,

Adams had studied at the Paris conservatoire and had composed over eighty operatic stage works, including his masterpiece, *Giselle*, in 1841. His fame soon led to requests to compose music all over the world. He had a good sense of what the public liked to hear and was a master at writing music for mass consumption.

Yet it wasn't the music so much that was the challenge for Adams. It was the fact that he was Jewish and the lyrics were decidedly Christian. How could he write music for a day he didn't observe, celebrating a Messiah he didn't believe was God's son? Despite the obstacles, he persevered and created a musical masterpiece, to the delight of both Cappeau and Father Petitjean.

Around the same time, a soprano opera singer, Emily Laurie, was in Roquemaure with her engineer husband, who was overseeing construction on a nearby bridge. Out of her friendship with Adams, she agreed to perform "Cantique de Noel" just three weeks later at the midnight Mass service on Christmas Eve.

The song became an instant hit, first among the locals before being more widely circulated in towns all over France. In the beginning, it was wholeheartedly accepted and embraced by the church and was a mainstay at countless Christmas Eve services.

For a short while, the song became less popular as the reputations of the author and composer were revealed. Furor developed among church leaders when they discovered Cappeau was an atheist and opposed to the power and influence of the church and that Adams was Jewish. The song was quickly and uniformly banned and declared unsuitable for Christmas services. It was deemed as lacking musical taste and absent of religious spirit. The church succeeded in burying the song for a while, but over time, the ordinary people of France refused to comply and continued to sing one of their favorite songs, only driving its popularity.

One reason for this might have something to do with the legend surrounding the song. The story goes that on Christmas Eve in 1871, during the Franco-Prussian War, the armies of France and Germany were in the midst of intense battle, fighting it out in the trenches. Suddenly, a French soldier jumped out of the trench with no weapon in hand and began singing "Cantique de Noel" only to be joined in song by a German infantryman. Singing broke out between both sides, and the fighting ceased for the next twenty-four hours as soldiers from both camps celebrated Christmas Day.

Another reason for the song's survival is that by 1855 a London publisher had translated it into many languages, making it widely available to new audiences around the world, including a reclusive American writer, John Sullivan Dwight, who put his own touch on the song.

Dwight graduated from Harvard College and Harvard University Divinity School, becoming a Unitarian minister in Northampton, Massachusetts. His occupation in pastoral ministry was cut short due to numerous panic attacks he suffered while speaking in front of congregations. Searching for a new line of work, he returned to his early love of music, and in 1852 launched *Dwight's Journal of Music*, a weekly periodical that became one of the most respected and influential such periodicals in the country. He edited the journal for thirty years and is widely considered the first American music critic.

In 1855 Dwight discovered "Cantique de Noel." He was inspired by the powerful lyrics about the birth of Christ, but he saw something else that corresponded to his abolitionist beliefs as the movement to outlaw slavery was heating up in the North. He translated the carol into English and made some adjustments to the lyrics, publishing it in his journal under the title "O Holy Night."

This new version quickly became a favorite among Christian abolitionists and was popular during the Civil War mainly because of the third verse: "Truly he taught us to love one another, his law is love and his gospel is peace, chains shall he break, for the slave is our brother, and in his name all oppression shall cease."

Over fifty years later—long after the Civil War had ended, when Cappeau and Dwight were old men and Adams had been dead for many years—the song broke historical ground when a university professor made "O Holy Night" the first song ever to be broadcast live on the radio.

Reginald Fessenden, a professor and inventor best known for his pioneering work developing radio technology, was experimenting in his office one Christmas Eve in 1906 with a microphone and a telegraph. At this time, the only radios that existed were wireless transmitters that picked up code. Fessenden proceeded to do something that had never been done before by broadcasting a human voice over the airwaves.

Speaking into a makeshift microphone, he recited the birth of Christ from Luke chapter 2 from his Bible. Then he picked up his violin and played "O Holy Night," making it the first song ever to be broadcast over the radio. Radio operators all over the world must have been stunned as the normal, coded impulses they would normally transcribe were miraculously altered into a man's voice and music.

Since that first debut broadcast, "O Holy Night" has become one of the music industry's most recorded and played songs. But more notably, since that first Christmas Eve in 1847, it's been sung millions of times in Christian churches worldwide.

How has this song, which battled multiple controversies and survived very nearly being banished from existence by the church, somehow reclaimed that much anticipated high point of the Christmas Eve celebration?

Perhaps it's because "O Holy Night" clearly embodies the redemptive aspects of the Christmas story, turning our hearts to the reason why we celebrate the birth of Jesus. It was a night like no other when our majestic and awesome God broke into our world in the form of a human baby to become our King. He was no ordinary King but rather a Savior sent to rescue us from a broken and sinful world. And in that moment and every Christmas Eve since, we, too, stand by his cradle on that holy night in awe of the Christ child.

It's interesting to wonder whether Father Petitjean would've had any idea that his simple request to the local town's atheist would eventually produce one of the most beautiful, inspired pieces of music ever created.

O Holy Night

O holy night, the stars are brightly shining,
It is the night of the dear Saviour's birth;
Long lay the world in sin and error pining,
Till he appeared and the soul felt its worth.
A thrill of hope the weary world rejoices,
For yonder breaks a new and glorious morn;

Fall on your knees,
Oh hear the angel voices!
O night divine! O night when Christ was born.
O night, O holy night, O night divine.

Led by the light of Faith serenely beaming;
With glowing hearts by his cradle we stand:
So, led by light of a star sweetly gleaming,
Here come the wise men from Orient land,
The King of Kings lay thus in lowly manger,
In all our trials born to be our friend;

He knows our need,
To our weakness no stranger!
Behold your King! Before Him lowly bend!
Behold your King! your King! before him bend!

Truly He taught us to love one another;
His law is Love and His gospel is Peace;
Chains shall he break, for the slave is our brother,
And in his name all oppression shall cease,
Sweet hymns of joy in grateful Chorus raise we;
Let all within us praise his Holy name!

Christ is the Lord,
then ever! ever praise we!
His pow'r and glory, evermore proclaim!
His pow'r and glory, evermore proclaim!

Cantique de Noël (Christmas Song)

Midnight, Christians, is the solemn hour,
When God as man descended unto us
To erase the stain of original sin
And to end the wrath of His Father.
The entire world thrills with hope
On this night that gives it a Saviour.

People, kneel down, await your deliverance.
Christmas, Christmas, here is the Redeemer,
Christmas, Christmas, here is the Redeemer!

May the ardent light of our Faith
Guide us all to the cradle of the infant,
As in ancient times a brilliant star
Guided the Oriental kings there.
The King of Kings was born in a humble manger;
O mighty ones of today, proud of your greatness,

It is to your pride that God preaches.
Bow your heads before the Redeemer!
Bow your heads before the Redeemer!

The Redeemer has broken every bond
The Earth is free, and Heaven is open.
He sees a brother where there was only a slave,
Love unites those whom iron had chained.
Who will tell Him of our gratitude,
For all of us He is born, He suffers and dies.

People, stand up! Sing of your deliverance,

Christmas, Christmas, sing of the Redeemer,
Christmas, Christmas, sing of the Redeemer!

Week 1, Day 2

THE NIGHT OF THE DEAR SAVIOR'S BIRTH

The light shines in the darkness, and the darkness has not overcome it. John 1:5

T he first day of winter is called the winter solstice, and it's an astronomical event in the Northern Hemisphere that can occur anywhere between December 20 and December 23. It's the one day of the year with the fewest hours of sunlight and the longest night, meaning it's the shortest and darkest day of the year.

For some, the onset of shorter, darker days can trigger a type of depression that saps their energy and makes them feel moody, giving them the "winter blues." There's even a clinical name for it: seasonal affective disorder. Science has shown that six percent of Americans suffer from this disorder in the winter months, with symptoms including poor concentration, over-sleeping, feelings of worthlessness, and weight gain. The gold standard treatment for it is exposure to light, and the brightest of lights are best.

While we think of Christmas as a season of light, the truth is, the birth story of Jesus Christ is not so much. God had been silent for four hundred years, leaving his people to walk in spiritual darkness. They were living under the oppressive rule of the Romans, and the nation of Israel was fracturing into various political groups that sought and fought to lead the people. Darkness permeated Judaism.

Then something truly incredible happened! Jesus came as the incarnate Word of God to bring the light of God's life into a spiritually dark and dying world. His light is powerful and far-reaching, able to illuminate and dispel the darkest of days. The nature of light is to shine, and darkness cannot exist in the presence of light. Despite whatever darkness is in the world or your life, it's important to remember that the Light of Jesus Christ cannot lose against the darkness; the darkness will never overcome it.

The reality of dark winters is not in itself comforting, but this year, begin to take notice of a very definite and subtle trend that begins around December 24 or 25. You'll find the days starting to get longer and the light returning! What provides the most comfort on any dark day is to remember that the light of Christ came on the darkest of nights to give us hope and to pour light into our hearts to shine out into our lives for others to see.

Week 1, Day 3

LONG LAY THE WORLD IN SIN AND ERROR PINING

For we know that the whole creation has been groaning together in the pains of childbirth until now. Romans 8:22

Y ou've probably sung this carol a hundred times, but have you ever wondered what the term "error pining" means? I hadn't...or at least until now. It's funny, but as I child, I remember singing it as "ever pining"...although I wouldn't have known what that meant either.

The first part of the verse, "Long lay the world in sin," is fairly self-explanatory in that from creation until the birth of Christ, the entire world lay cursed after Adam's sin. But the term "error pining" adds another, more fatal descriptor about the state of the fallen world.

Pine is a verb with two different meanings. Today, we might use the word pine to refer to the longing or yearning after something unattainable. For example, we might say, "Stop pining after what you don't have, and be grateful for what you do." But the context used in this verse is derived from the Old English *pinian*, which meant to torment, cause to suffer, afflict, punish, or have feelings of regret. So in this case, "error pining" alludes to a world languishing in regret over sin before the appearance of Christ.

This is often where we find ourselves—pining away after lesser things that never seem to satisfy the soul and ultimately lead to regret and despair. Unfortunately, it's often never more evident than during the Christmas season. A recent statistic states that over 40% of Americans are willing to go into debt buying Christmas presents if it makes them or their family happy in the moment. Research further shows that a good majority of those same buyers end up regretting their purchases later when the bills come due.

Paul compares this pining to a creation groaning for the day when at last sin is removed and all of nature will burst forth in glory. That "groaning" is so intense that he uses the metaphor of the pains of childbirth to describe it. You and I are part of this dire assessment of a world that groans for something better but often refuses to recognize the one who can truly provide it.

C.S. Lewis famously wrote, "If we find ourselves with a desire that nothing in this world can satisfy, the most probable explanation is that we were made for another world." That other world is where Jesus came from before being born into ours. It's also a place that He longs to bring us to and promises to do so for those who love and trust him.

Perhaps this Christmas, we can remove the "error" in front of "pining" and simply pine after the one who guarantees a satisfied life with no regrets to those who do.

Week 1, Day 4

FOR YONDER BREAKS A NEW AND GLORIOUS MORN

But this I call to mind, and therefore I have hope: The steadfast love of the Lord never ceases; his mercies never come to an end; they are new every morning; great is your faithfulness. Lamentations 3:21–23

D o you remember that feeling on Christmas Eve of being so excited as a kid that you couldn't sleep? The next morning seemed so far away, and you couldn't wait to experience the thrill of opening presents, attending church, eating a big family breakfast, or loading up the car to visit family. Christmas morning can mean different things to different people, but what if every morning felt like Christmas morning? What if, regardless of what was happening in your life, you could bottle that feeling of hope and excitement for the next morning to experience each night before going to bed?

This is exactly what the prophet Jeremiah, who wrote the book of Lamentations, did. Jeremiah is often referred to as the weeping prophet, and his book is widely considered the saddest one in the Bible. If you're wondering why, just randomly pick a few verses, and you'll quickly gain an understanding as to why your pastor never preaches on it. Jeremiah wrote the book while grieving and mourning the destruction of the once great city of Jerusalem by the Babylonians in 586 BC.

In his lament, Jeremiah does not hold back but rather lists all of his struggles and afflictions, fully admitting that life is full of pain and difficulty. This continues chapter after chapter, verse after verse, until suddenly his tone changes as he finds something that gives him hope: Christmas morning!

It might seem as though my interpretation of this Scripture passage is a bit off, but let me explain. Through all of Jeremiah's toils and problems, what gave him hope was knowing without a doubt that God loves, shows compassion, and is faithful. And in the birth of Jesus Christ, we have the fullest expression of all three of these attributes. God loved us so much and had so much compassion for the horrible state that we were in that He was faithful to his promise of sending a Savior to rescue us. Jeremiah held on to that promise, and it's what gave him hope during the worst days of his life.

What if each night we acted as if the next morning were Christmas Day? What if we woke up each morning confident of God's endless love and never-ending compassion for and faithfulness to us? I believe this passage holds some of the most comforting and reassuring words you will find in the Bible, and if put into practice, they will provide hope through some of the darkest days.

Week 1, Day 5

FALL ON YOUR KNEES! OH HEAR THE ANGEL VOICES!

But when Simon Peter saw it, he fell down at Jesus'
knees, saying, "Depart from me, for I am a sinful
man, O Lord." Luke 5:8

Throughout Jesus' ministry, we see many examples of those falling on their knees in desperation before Him, including lepers, officials, moms, dads, the demon possessed, and many others who desired healing for themselves or someone else. Culturally, bowing at the feet of another was common practice in the ancient world as a sign of submission, honor, and respect. Historically, it was also a sign of surrender during times of war.

"O Holy Night" is one of the most powerful carols we sing at Christmastime. The music composition has huge swells that carry you to the place where you want to "fall on your knees" as the angels announce and proclaim the birth of Jesus. The visual is really quite dramatic. It's more than merely bowing your head or even kneeling. The definition of "fall" is to move rapidly downward. The idea put forth here is an extravagant or elaborate display, an expression of praise, adoration, respect, reverence, and, yes, even feelings of unworthiness.

Peter had a similar experience shortly after meeting Jesus. After an unsuccessful night of fishing and catching nothing at all, Jesus instructed Peter to let down his nets again. To his surprise, the catch was so enormous that the nets began to break and threatened to sink two boats! As Peter felt the weight of trying to drag this miraculous catch of fish on board, he became more acutely aware of the weight of his own sin and unworthiness. His first response was to fall before Jesus, claiming he was unworthy to be a part of any of this. Interestingly, as Peter was trying to push Jesus away, Jesus actually pulled him closer and invited Peter to be one of the twelve disciples!

Have you ever felt unworthy in the presence of God? If so, you're in good company. So did Moses, Isaiah, Gideon, and many others, including Mary, who, when told that she would be the mother of the Messiah, humbly questioned how it could be so. Often it's when we're in the presence of God that we become acutely aware of our own sin and unworthiness. It's also a time when we're most likely to fall to our knees before him or even try to push him away. Fortunately for us, his hold is stronger!

This Christmas, as you reflect on the great hope that the birth of Christ brings and any feelings of unworthiness that you may have, you're invited to fall on your knees in awe and praise while rejoicing with the angels, giving glory to God in the highest.

Week 1, Day 6

TRULY HE TAUGHT US TO LOVE ONE ANOTHER

"A new commandment I give to you, that you love one another: just as I have loved you, you also are to love one another. By this all people will know that you are my disciples, if you have love for one another." John 13:34–35

The classic Christmas movie, *It's a Wonderful Life*, chronicles the life of George Bailey—an average middle-aged man living a normal life in a small-town community. As a young man, George bragged that he would "shake off the dust of this crummy little town" and get away to see the world and achieve great things. Yet through tragedy and his own sense of responsibility, he ends up spending his entire life in a town he desperately wanted to escape from.

One Christmas Eve, when George stands accused of fraud and is at his lowest point, he receives a visit from an angel who enables him to see what life would have been like had he never lived. It's a battle between good and evil, selflessness and selfishness, and it's a story of faith, family, and friends. It's the story of loving others so much that you would give up your self-interest for theirs even when it costs you everything—maybe even your life. This, of course, makes it the perfect Christmas movie and a wonderful demonstration of selfless love.

It's a Wonderful Life is not so much about the intrinsic value of each individual life but about how that life touches so many other lives around it. Jesus taught that his people would be known by their love and that we are to love in the same way that He loves us. And how does God love us? According to Romans 5:8, God demonstrated his own love for us by clothing himself in the flesh of a man on that first Christmas Day and then, while we were still sinners, dying for us.

George did not always find it easy to love others, and neither do we. Loving others can be extremely difficult at times, mainly due to sin—both ours and that of those we try to love. Apart from God's grace, we are selfish people who tend to find loving our own self-interests easier than that of others. But love is not selfish; it's patient and kind.

George Bailey was known for his love of his neighbors and had a wonderful life because it was spent in service to them. He was not perfect, and he made mistakes, even one that almost cost him his life. However, in the end, he found that his sacrifice for others resulted in their sacrifice for him. He truly had a wonderful life, a life that no amount of money can buy. I can think of no better movie to watch at Christmas.

CHAINS SHALL HE BREAK, FOR THE SLAVE IS OUR BROTHER

The Spirit of the Lord is upon me, because he has anointed me to proclaim good news to the poor. He has sent me to proclaim liberty to the captives and recovering of sight to the blind, to set at liberty those who are oppressed. Luke 4:18

Known as the "Moses of her people," Harriet Tubman was born into a life of slavery in 1822 but escaped to Philadelphia in 1849. Once free, she helped others gain their freedom as an operator of the Underground Railroad—a network of people, places, and routes that provided shelter and assistance to escaping slaves. She went on thirteen different missions on the Underground Railroad, mostly directed toward her own family and friends, but many others also found their freedom due to her efforts.

It was also during this turbulent time that John Dwight Sullivan became particularly inspired by a French Christmas carol as it corresponded with his abolitionist beliefs. When he translated the carol into English, he took special care with the third verse. A fairly direct translation of the original French version reads,

"He sees a brother where there was only a slave. Love unites those that iron had chained." Dwight changed it to the rousing lines, "Chains shall He break for the slave is our brother, and in His name all oppression shall cease." This new version quickly became a favorite among Christian abolitionists during the time of Tubman and Sullivan and was also popular during the Civil War.

"O Holy Night" is more than just your normal Christmas carol. It gives meaning to the cause against the evils of slavery and oppression by connecting it with the most incredible news ever—the birth of Christ. Jesus came to a world searching for freedom and peace. He came to those in captivity, the hurting, and the lost. To those who were without hope, yearning for salvation. He came to bring freedom in every capacity.

Christmas is about freedom, about breaking chains, whether physical, emotional, or spiritual. This is good news, and all Christians should take up the mantle of Christ and proclaim this news to the poor, to those who are faint in spirit, to the hurting and lost, and to those no longer desiring to be a captive of sin.

It's probably as true for you as it was for me that in all the times I've sung this carol, the abolitionist sentiments of this verse never entered my mind. Perhaps it was because I didn't know the history, but I can almost imagine Tubman and her fellow escaped slaves singing it on their journey to freedom. This Christmas, as you belt out this verse, meditate on the freedom of all mankind from the sin that enslaves them. Then be reminded of the brokenhearted, the hurting, and the lost around you as you proclaim His good news.

"I HEARD THE BELLS ON CHRISTMAS DAY": A HISTORY

"I Heard the Bells on Christmas Day" is generally not the first carol to be requested while sipping eggnog around a roaring fire with family and friends. In fact, most people probably don't know many of the words, yet they fully recognize the hymn and hum along when they hear it. In this carol, you'll find no holly, tinsel, or beautiful imagery of the birth of the Christ child. It certainly doesn't scream yuletide, but it's real, it's raw, and it's born out of the painful circumstances of one of the most famous poets of his day.

Henry Wadsworth Longfellow was a famed nineteenth century scholar, novelist, and poet, known for works like "Paul Revere's Ride," "Evangeline," and "The Song of Hiawatha." He was born in Portland, Maine (then still part of Massachusetts) on February 27, 1807, to an established New England family. He was the second son in a family of eight children. His mother, Zilpah Wadsworth, was the daughter of a Revolutionary War hero. His father, Stephen Longfellow, was a prominent Portland lawyer and later a member of Congress.

Longfellow attended Portland Academy and Bowdoin College, graduating in 1825. He then studied modern languages in Europe for three years before returning to Bowdoin as a teacher and then later as a professor at Harvard. In 1831 he married Mary Potter, a childhood friend from Portland. A few years later, while traveling overseas, she died from complications of a miscarriage. Her death deeply saddened Longfellow, as reflected in his writings during that period.

In 1839 he met Frances (Fanny) Appleton, the daughter of a Boston industrialist, and after years of courting, she finally agreed to marry him in 1843. They had an exceptionally happy marriage, providing Longfellow with the domestic stability that he had missed and producing six children.

They settled down in the historic Craigie House overlooking the Charles River in Cambridge, Massachusetts. A wedding present from his father-in-law, the Craigie House was once the headquarters of George Washington during the siege of Boston. In 1854 Longfellow retired from Harvard, devoting himself entirely to writing.

Tragedy struck in the Longfellow home on July 9, 1861. His wife, Fanny, was sitting in the library with their two little girls, Edith and Allegra. After trimming some of seven-year-old Edith's beautiful curls, Fanny decided to preserve the clippings in small packages by melting a bar of hot sealing wax with a candle to secure it. It's thought at some point that a few drops of the hot wax fell unnoticed upon her summer dress just as a breeze gusted through an open window, igniting the light material and engulfing her in flames.

Longfellow, sleeping in the next room, was awakened by her screams as Fanny ran into his study to protect Edith and Allegra. He frantically tried to extinguish the flames with an undersized throw rug before throwing his own body on her in a desperate attempt to smoother the flames. Tragically, by the time the fire was out, Fanny had already suffered severe burns. A doctor was called, but her burns were beyond recovery. After falling in and out of consciousness throughout the night, Fanny died the next morning, just a couple of days before their eighteenth wedding anniversary.

Longfellow was severely burned on his face, arms, and hands while trying to save Fanny, which left him too sick to attend her funeral a few days later. His face became so scarred from the burns that he was unable to shave, so he wore a beard from then on, which became his trademark.

This horribly traumatic way in which he lost his wife marked a turning point in Longfellow's life. His physical wounds healed, but his suffering and grief mounted and he sank into a depression. His physical appearance changed dramatically as he grew a long beard to hide his scars, and at times, he feared they would send him to an asylum on account of his grief.

Over the next couple of years, his work also suffered as he spent much of his time translating other works and less on his own creation. He would record in his journal on the Christmas after Fanny's death, "I can make no record of these days. Better leave them wrapped in silence. Perhaps someday God will give me peace." The following year on Christmas Day in 1862 he wrote, "'A merry Christmas,' say the children, but that is no more for me."

To add further to his grief, just a few months later, in March 1863, his eighteen-year-old son Charley, against his father's wishes, left the family home and boarded a train traveling four hundred miles to Washington, DC, to join the Union army to fight in the Civil War. Longfellow was a staunch abolitionist but, like the rest of the country, was fully aware of how brutal and bloody the war had become and the tragedy that could befall his son.

Charley, though, eager to do his part, joined and quickly became a Second Lieutenant, probably due to his influential ties or his father's lobbying efforts for his son to become an officer. He was at the Battle of Chancellorsville in Virginia but spent his time guarding wagons, seeing no combat. Shortly thereafter, he came down with typhoid fever and was sent home for several months to recover, narrowly dodging the Battle of Gettysburg that July. By August 1863 he had rejoined his unit and was back in the fight, but his luck was beginning to run out.

On November 27, 1863, while involved in a skirmish during a battle of the Mine Run Campaign, Charley was shot through the left shoulder, with the bullet exiting under his right shoulder blade. The bullet had traveled across his back and nicked his spine. His injury was severe, and they transported him to a hospital in Washington, DC.

Longfellow was dining home alone on December 1 when a telegram arrived, inaccurately stating that his son had been shot in the face and was near death. Immediately, he set out for DC with Ernest, Charley's younger brother, in search of his elder son. He found him five days later in a hospital and was informed by the army surgeon of the actual injury and that his son narrowly avoided being paralyzed by less than an inch. He took Charley back home to recover, arriving at the Cambridge house on December 8. Despite his wish to return to the battlefield, Charley was soon honorably discharged.

On Christmas Day, just two weeks after bringing his son home, Longfellow—as a fifty-seven-year-old widowed father of six children—heard the optimistic sounds of Christmas bells ringing over Cambridge, announcing peace on Earth and goodwill to men. But how could he believe that? He had lost his wife in a tragic and horrifying death and just brought his injured and almost paralyzed son back from a gruesome war that was still raging on and tearing the country apart.

The circumstances of what he was hearing with his ears and what he felt in his heart challenged him to write a poem. As he wrote, he discovered a deeper message in the bells in that there will be moments of life filled with grief and despair, but God is alive, and his righteousness will prevail in the end.

The poem originally contained seven stanzas, and he titled it "Christmas Bells." It was first published in February 1865 in *Our Young Folks*, a juvenile magazine, and by 1872 it was put to music by the English organist John Baptiste Calkin for a processional, set to the melody of "Waltham." Two stanzas containing references to the American Civil War were omitted, thus giving us the carol in its present form. In 1956 Jewish American songwriter Johnny Marks composed another melody, which became very popular with a variety of recording artists, from Bing Crosby to Casting Crowns.

Longfellow's questioning of the existence of peace on Earth is certainly understandable. Even now, it's easy to examine the world around us and wonder the same thing. But the louder and deeper Longfellow's Christmas bells rang, the more they reminded him that God is not dead or asleep. He is alive, and one day our resurrected Savior will right all the wrongs and truly bring peace to rule the Earth.

I Heard the Bells on Christmas Day

I heard the bells on Christmas day
Their old familiar carols play,
And wild and sweet the words repeat
Of peace on earth, good will to men.

I thought how, as the day had come,
The belfries of all Christendom
Had rolled along th'unbroken song
Of peace on earth, good will to men.

And in despair I bowed my head:
"There is no peace on earth," I said,
"For hate is strong, and mocks the song
Of peace on earth, good will to men."

Then pealed the bells more loud and deep:
"God is not dead, nor doth He sleep;
The wrong shall fail, the right prevail,
With peace on earth, good will to men."

Till, ringing, singing on its way,
The world revolved from night to day
A voice, a chime, a chant sublime,
Of peace on earth, good will to men.

Christmas Bells – Longfellow Version

I heard the bells on Christmas Day
Their old, familiar carols play,
And wild and sweet, The words repeat
Of peace on earth, good-will to men!

And thought how, as the day had come,
The belfries of all Christendom
Had rolled along, The unbroken song
Of peace on earth, good-will to men!

Till ringing, singing on its way,
The world revolved from night to day,
A voice, a chime, A chant sublime
Of peace on earth, good-will to men!

Then from each black, accursed mouth
The cannon thundered in the South,
And with the sound, The carols drowned
Of peace on earth, good-will to men!

It was as if an earthquake rent
The hearth-stones of a continent,
And made forlorn, The households born
Of peace on earth, good-will to men!

And in despair I bowed my head;
"There is no peace on earth," I said;
"For hate is strong, And mocks the song
Of peace on earth, good-will to men!"

Then pealed the bells more loud and deep:

"God is not dead, nor doth He sleep;
The Wrong shall fail, The Right prevail,
With peace on earth, good-will to men."

Week 2, Day 9

THE OLD FAMILIAR CAROLS PLAY

These people honor me with their lips, but their heart is far from me. Mark 7:6

Quickly becoming a holiday classic, the warm and engaging comedy film *Christmas with the Kranks* tells the story of a couple who skip Christmas one year since their daughter is traveling abroad. They selfishly take all the money normally spent celebrating Christmas and decide to take a luxury cruise instead. This doesn't sit well with their Christmas-obsessed neighbors, who are determined to win the best decorated street competition, as they have each year. The Kranks soon find themselves the recipients of neighborhood scorn when they refuse to get in the seasonal spirit.

We, too, can elicit feelings of excitement and nostalgia just thinking about Christmas. We smell the cookies baking, we hear the joyous sounds of carols, and our eyes become resplendent by bright, festive lights. Such sensory exuberance helps create lasting recollections of those occasions and marks them in our memories as special events worth cherishing. These events often end up producing pleasant, yearly traditions that we count on each year to draw us into the Christmas spirit.

And why shouldn't we love our memories and traditions when you consider that everyday life is so stressful and full of uncertainty? Research shows that traditions can provide various psychological benefits, helping us enjoy ourselves, uniting us with those we love, and providing stability during times of stress and transition. And families that celebrate repeated traditions report stronger emotional connections and unity than families that don't.

But just as traditions can enrich our lives, they also can become a burden as we find ourselves bent low under the heavy load of our own expectations of the season. We feel a sense of obligation to do things a certain way, and when it doesn't happen just right, we're left with feelings of guilt. We become like the Kranks' neighbors, robbing ourselves of the joy of the season because we're following some unalterable holiday script.

It was in this burden of tradition that the Pharisees and scribes confronted Jesus about his disciples not washing their hands before eating. He had sharp words for them, saying their traditions did not honor God at all because their hearts were far from him.

Neither the Kranks nor their neighbors were exhibiting true Christmas spirit. One was focused on abandoning all tradition, while the others were taking it to the extreme. When our traditions draw our hearts near to God, they're worth keeping—like the old familiar carols that remind us of the Christ child and his reason for coming. But when traditions distract us from the true purpose of Christmas, then perhaps it's time to abandon them.

Week 2, Day 10

THERE IS NO PEACE ON EARTH I SAID

But as he considered these things, behold, an angel of the Lord appeared to him in a dream, saying, "Joseph, son of David, do not fear to take Mary as your wife, for that which is conceived in her is from the Holy Spirit. She will bear a son, and you shall call his name Jesus, for he will save his people from their sins." Matthew 1:20–21

W hen the church bells rang out jubilantly that Christmas morning, Longfellow felt a disconnect between what he was hearing and the realities of what he was experiencing at that moment in his life. Not only was he struggling with personal tragedy but he was living in a nation engulfed in war, having just seen one of the bloodiest battles yet at the Battle of Gettysburg, with more than fifty thousand estimated casualties. As he sat down to write this verse, he seemed to be questioning that if Jesus was indeed the Prince of Peace, where was that peace?

Joseph's first introduction to the Prince of Peace was also anything but peaceful. When finding out that the woman he was engaged to be married to was pregnant and he was not the father, what else could he believe but that she had been unfaithful to him? He was shocked, angry, and depressed—it's how anyone would react in that situation. It appeared Mary had violated what, at the time, was considered a legally binding agreement and a sacred trust between them. By law, she was already his wife and, as such, could be accused of adultery, which was punishable by death.

But Joseph was a compassionate man, and even though he felt hurt and betrayed, he had no interest in bringing greater shame on Mary or her family and decided to divorce her quietly. Why should he let her shame extend to him? He'd done nothing wrong. As difficult of a decision as it was, he decided it was the right one.

That fretful night, as he tossed and turned in bed, void of any peace, something miraculous happened. An angel of the Lord showed up in his dream with a clear message: The baby conceived in Mary was miraculously given from the Holy Spirit, and for that reason, he should not be afraid to take her as his wife. Oh, and by the way, she will bear a son and you, Joseph, are to name him Jesus and he will save his people from their sins.

Joseph might not have woken that morning with perfect peace, but he was bold and courageous, trusting in God even when he didn't understand everything that was going on. In fact, the next couple of years would be incredibly difficult for Joseph, Mary, and Jesus. But perfect peace isn't dependent on circumstances; it comes from a steadfast heart trusting in God regardless of those circumstances.

Christmas can be a great source of stress for many and, at various times of our lives, not all that peaceful. But no matter what your circumstances may be, remember that while situations in this life may cause us stress, the only way to find true peace is by focusing our attention on Christ and his great love for us.

Week 2, Day 11

FOR HATE IS STRONG AND MOCKS THE SONG

If the world hates you, know that it has hated me before it hated you. John 15:18

The word hate is tossed around a lot in our culture today and has become an overused word or label given to anyone you disagree with. For Longfellow, it meant something entirely different. As he wrote this verse, he was a troubled man living in a truly hateful and broken world filled with pain and death as the result of a gruesome war. He saw neighbor killing neighbor over the enslavement of another. As he reflected in that moment on his thoughts, hate appeared too strong and would always outweigh the good in the world.

There are days when you might feel this way and, in holiday exasperation, erroneously cry out, "I hate Christmas." In your frustration, you're not expressing some deep hatred for Jesus, the nativity, the shepherds, or the wisemen. What you're really meaning to say is, "This time of year stresses me out." However, that's not to say Jesus is not hated. The fact is, no one has ever been the object of more hatred than Jesus and his followers.

From the announcement of his birth, King Herod hated the thought of the Messiah so much that he had every baby boy under two years of age slaughtered in Bethlehem. Then, at his death, those Jesus came to love and save responded to that love with hatred, shouting, "Crucify him!"

Jesus warned the first century disciples, just as he warns us today, following him means also sharing his lot, being rejected, and even being hated by "the world" because our values are different. We should expect no different treatment than what our Savior received, but our efforts should never be deterred. Instead, we should emulate the hated and despised shepherds, who, after witnessing the birth of the Christ child, became the first evangelists, telling everyone they met about what they had seen, all the while praising God.

This Christmas you're not likely to be jeered at by an Ebeneezer Scrooge-like character who chastised the poor caroling child who came singing at his door, "God Rest Ye Merry Gentleman." In fact, most of us will never experience the level of persecution and hatred that many of those first century believers would endure in their lives.

Imagine for a moment those hated shepherds running up and down the streets of Bethlehem, excited beyond belief to share the joy that was within them with no thought of what others might think. May we be just as bold this Christmas and overcome any hate by sharing that same joy of the birth of Jesus through ordinary acts of love and care for others.

GOD IS NOT DEAD NOR DOTH HE SLEEP

Have this mind among yourselves, which is yours in Christ Jesus, who, though he was in the form of God, did not count equality with God a thing to be grasped, but emptied himself, by taking the form of a servant, being born in the likeness of men. And being found in human form, he humbled himself by becoming obedient to the point of death, even death on a cross. Philippians 2:5–8

Human beings are built with limits. We're limited by space in that we can only be in one place at one time. We're limited in knowledge in that our brains can only absorb finite amounts of information. We're limited in wisdom in that our insights and judgment are subject to our own experiences. And we're limited in physical ability in that our bodies require sleep to operate efficiently but still have a limited lifespan.

God has no limitations. Scripture teaches us that Jesus was entirely God and never ceased being God when born into this world as a human baby that first Christmas. But his mission was to provide us with the perfect example of humanity, so he voluntarily chose to restrict the use of his divinity and became just like us—with all the same limitations and sufferings we experience but with one major exception: He overcame the world.

When Christ said he overcame the world, he meant he had defeated sin and the enemy. He had defeated death. And because Jesus overcame the world, we are overcomers too as we embrace him in faith.

This is important to remember because amid the storms of life in a dark and fallen world, we begin to question God's goodness, love, and care for us. It's a very natural response when examining the suffering in everyday life to question the existence of an all-knowing, loving God.

God, however, doesn't always offer us the answers we seek. In this life, we might never really understand why some things have happened. But as we draw closer to him, we, too, can overcome those deep, dark days. He longs for us to come to him, talk to him, and bring our suffering to him.

German poet and philosopher Friedrich Nietzsche is most famous for making the statement, "God is dead," in the late 1800s. But God is not dead nor is he asleep at the helm of this world. He is very much alive. Though the whole world may rage, he holds it in his hand and stands firmly in eternity, working his plan to make all things new.

Be reminded the next time you sing this verse that regardless of what's going on in your life or the chaotic world around you, God is still at work and will never leave us, even in our deepest hurts or in the darkest moments. He is always there.

THE WRONG SHALL FAIL, THE RIGHT PREVAIL

And Jesus came and said to them, "All authority in heaven and on earth has been given to me."
Matthew 28:18

Ray Bradbury's 1962 fantasy novel, *Something Wicked This Way Comes*, concerns a mysterious carnival outside a small town in the early 1900s that grants the wishes of the town's citizens with dark consequences. Mr. Dark, the carnival's proprietor, first appears in the story putting up carnival posters while singing, "I Heard the Bells on Christmas Day," in particular a line about how good will prevail over evil.

Mr. Dark is the wicked antagonist of the novel, and later it's revealed that he knows Scripture very well as he simultaneously tosses the Bible in a trash can. Despite it being a strange tune for an evil character to be singing, since the song promises that the "wrong shall fail," it actually underscores the plot structure of the entire book that right will ultimately prevail.

But isn't this the plot structure of every good story where you have the juxtaposition of good and evil? There are common elements to every extraordinary story, including the protagonist, or the hero of the story, and the antagonist, who represents the villain. There's some event or action that sets the characters into motion that presents a conflict, challenge, quest, or mystery that draws the reader into the story further. Finally, it all leads to the resolution or climax where we find out who finally wins, and in most stories that we enjoy, good prevails and evil fails.

When we think about the birth of Christ, all of these story elements come into play. We have Jesus as our protagonist and Satan as the antagonist. Jesus' birth in Bethlehem sets into motion a series of events that lead us all the way to the climax at the cross, where evil seems to have won. Then, three days later, when all seems to have been lost, our protagonist rises, defeats evil for good, and claims comprehensive authority over all creation.

With this authority, he is always in control, even when it seems to be to the contrary. He declares authority over nature as he calms the storms in our lives. He declares authority over sickness and disease when he makes the blind to see, deaf to hear, and lame to walk. He declares authority over the devil and demons as he rebukes them and they flee. Finally, he declared authority over death when he defeated sin and rose from the grave.

Ultimately, evil knows that it has no power over Good, but like Mr. Dark in Bradbury's epic story, it does not stop it from trying. Like Longfellow, we are invited this Advent to listen to the bell ringers testifying to God's presence and promises as we long for and anticipate that the wrong shall fail once and for all and the right prevail for all eternity with peace forevermore.

Week 2, Day 14

PEACE ON EARTH GOOD WILL TO MEN

And suddenly there was with the angel a multitude of the heavenly host praising God and saying, "Glory to God in the highest, and on earth peace among those with whom he is pleased!" Luke 2:13–14

"Sure, Charlie Brown, I can tell you what Christmas is all about," Linus confidently pronounces as he walks to the center of the stage, calls for the lights, and recites the King James translation of Luke 2:8–14. For many of us, it was tradition to gather around the television set each year to watch the one airing of *A Charlie Brown Christmas* and to hear Linus once again tell us the meaning of Christmas.

The few short words that conclude Linus's stirring speech to his friends, "peace on Earth, goodwill to men," are synonymous with Christmas. Not only did an animated character drill it into our memories each year but we find it on greeting cards, in carols, and on Christmas decorations. And why not? The hopeful phrase conveys for many a spirit of generosity and a kindly disposition toward others.

The phrase is taken from the original King James translation, which declares peace and goodwill to all men. However, most modern translations more accurately connect the "peace and goodwill" with a certain group: "those with whom he is pleased." There's a major difference here. One translation is external and wishful thinking, connecting world peace and God's benevolence to all humanity. The other appears to be more internal with a personal message of reconciliation and hope, connecting that longing in our hearts for a peace that transcends any kind of earthly peace we seek—one that only Christ can give by accepting him as your Savior.

Interestingly, the story goes that network executives were not supportive of the scripture being quoted in the animated show. They assumed children would become bored. Charlie Brown creator Charles Schulz, however, was adamant that it remain. "If we don't tell the true meaning of Christmas, who will?" he asked. Fortunately, Schulz was the beneficiary of a tight production schedule, and the show's sponsor, Coca-Cola, had already begun promotion. The show went forward with Scripture included, and CBS executives were certain that it would be a ratings disaster. To their surprise, fifty percent of American television sets tuned in, and the soon to be classic was a tremendous success.

Linus's readings from the Bible lasted less than a minute but inspired Charlie Brown to pick up his fragile tree and walk out of the auditorium renewed. Whether you're searching for external peace in the chaotic world around you or internal peace for the turmoil within, it often begins with having "good will" toward those around you. Charlie Brown found that "peace and good will" in Linus's recitation of the Christmas story. Perhaps that is why Longfellow passionately included the phrase at the end of each stanza: to remind us "what Christmas is all about."

"O LITTLE TOWN OF BETHLEHEM": A HISTORY

P hillips Brooks was a giant of a man, standing six feet eight inches tall and weighing over three hundred pounds. Today he would seem a better fit as an NFL defensive lineman than playing with children on the floor in the church's nursery, but that was often where Brooks found himself. Just as great in his physical proportions, he also had a loving heart to match that endeared him to the old and young alike.

Brooks was born in Boston in 1835 to a long line of Puritan ancestors. He was raised in the strict ways of the evangelical wing of the Episcopal Church and educated at a Latin school and then Harvard University, from which he graduated in 1855. After an unsuccessful occupation as a schoolteacher, he entered the ministry and studied at Alexandria Seminary in Virginia, being ordained as an Episcopal priest in 1859.

Following ordination, he came to Philadelphia to become the pastor of a small church. It wasn't long before the natural enthusiasm that filled his sermons garnered the attention of others. Just two years later, in 1861, he was called to a new congregation in one of the fastest-growing, more fashionable areas of Philadelphia, Church of the Holy Trinity, where he served until 1869.

Brooks was a dynamic preacher and, while still in his twenties, rose in prominence, gaining national recognition for several sermons that he gave during the Civil War. He was a fervent supporter of the Union and the abolition of slavery, preaching forcibly against it. His most notable sermon, given two weeks after the assassination of President Lincoln, eulogized the President and the soldiers that gave their lives in the war. The popular sermon was reprinted and widely distributed across the Union. As for many in that time, the war was particularly personal for Brooks, having lost his younger brother, George, who died of typhoid pneumonia while serving in the Union Army.

In the war's aftermath and in need of some well-deserved rest, Brooks embarked on a year-long sabbatical, traveling through Europe and the Holy Land. On Christmas Eve in 1865, he mounted a horse and rode from Jerusalem to the still small village of Bethlehem. By nightfall he was in the field where, according to tradition, the shepherds heard the angelic announcement. In a letter he wrote to his father about the experience, he said, "Before dark we rode out of town to the field where they say the shepherds saw the star. It is a fenced piece of ground with a cave in it...somewhere in those fields we rode through...the shepherds were still 'keeping watch over their flocks,' or leading them home to fold."

Later that same evening, he attended the Christmas Eve service at the Church of the Nativity in Bethlehem, built over a cave considered the traditional site of the nativity. The entire service lasted for five hours, from 10 p.m. to 3 a.m. He would later write to the children of his parish about his visit to Bethlehem on Christmas Eve:

I remember especially on Christmas Eve, when I was standing in the old church at Bethlehem, close to the spot where Jesus was born, when the whole church was ringing hour after hour with the splendid hymns of praise to God, how again and again it seemed as if I could hear voices that I knew well, telling each other of the "Wonderful Night" of the Savior's birth.

In September 1866 Brooks returned to Philadelphia and to his congregation at the Church of the Holy Trinity, but his memory of that wonderful experience in Bethlehem and the sequence of events surrounding that one special Christmas Eve stayed with him. Little did he know it would provide the backdrop for one of the most popular Christmas carols of all time.

Two years later, in 1868, just prior to Christmas, Brooks wrote five verses about his Bethlehem experience that were to be performed by the children's choir for the Christmas Eve service. To set his words to music, Brooks turned to the church organist, Lewis Redner, to compose a simple melody for the children to sing on Christmas Eve.

A wealthy real estate broker by trade, Lewis Redner was very involved with local charities and served on the board of the Rescue Mission, the YMCA, and a home for children orphaned by the Civil War. Philanthropy was a passion of his but so was his great love for religious music. He had no formal music training but played the organ at four different churches during his life, spending nineteen of those years as the organist at Church of the Holy Trinity.

As the story goes, Brooks approached Redner with a simple little carol he had written for the children to sing at the Christmas Eve service and asked him to write the tune to it. Redner sat down at the piano and, for days, couldn't find the right tune to carry such descriptive words. When Brooks came to him the Friday before Sunday's Christmas Eve service to inquire of its status, Redner informed him he didn't have it but assured him he would by Sunday.

On Saturday evening, feeling frustrated and defeated, Redner went to bed, still having nothing to show Brooks the next day. During that fretful night, as Redner described it, "I was roused from sleep late in the night hearing an angel whispering the tune in my ear. I seized a piece of music paper and jotted down the melody of the tune as we now have it, and on Sunday morning before going to church I filled in the harmony."

There were some additional changes Redner made, including omitting the third verse altogether from the carol. His concern was over one line, which included the phrase, "Son of the undefiled," believing it might run into some controversy with the doctrine of the immaculate conception. Otherwise, the lyrics from Brooks and the melody Redner wrote are just as we sing it today.

Joyfully, he presented the tune to Brooks, claiming it was a gift from heaven. On Christmas Eve 1868, "O Little Town of Bethlehem" was sung for the first time by the children's choir.

The tune quickly became a favorite when a local bookstore printed the hymn on leaflets for sale. But it wasn't until six years later, in 1874, when Dr. Huntington, rector of All Saints' Church in Worcester, Massachusetts, asked permission to publish it in his hymnal called *The Church Porch*. It was he who christened Redner's music with the title "Saint Louis."

Gradually the carol became more popular with those connected within the Episcopal Church, and by 1890 it had made its appearance in various hymnals intended for church worship. It wasn't until 1892, twenty-four years after its first performance, that Brooks' carol was given a place in the official hymnal of his own denomination.

As the carol gained in universal popularity, other composers tried their hand at writing music for Brooks' lyrics. In the 1903 "Forest Green" version, composer Ralph Vaughan Williams set the lyrics to the tune of "The Ploughboy's Dream," a traditional English ballad that is still sung throughout Great Britain and Ireland.

In 1869 Brooks left Church of the Holy Trinity in Philadelphia to become the pastor of Trinity Church in Boston, where he served until being elected bishop of the Episcopal Church in Massachusetts in 1891. He was one of the most famous preachers of his generation in America and the preacher who introduced Helen Keller to Christianity. His unexpected death in 1893 was a major event in the history of Boston. One observer reported, "They buried him like a king. Harvard students carried his body on their shoulders. All barriers of denomination were down. Roman Catholics and Unitarians felt that a great man had fallen in Israel." They erected a statue of him at his church, and the Episcopal Church still remembers Brooks on January 23, the anniversary of his death.

For Redner, there were no statues erected nor did he experience the fame or have the dominating presence of Brooks. For that matter, he really wasn't an outstanding composer either—he wrote other Christmas and Easter carols that have largely been forgotten. Outside of being a successful businessman, Redner was just an average person and a good musician who agreed when asked by his pastor to write a tune for a poem for the Christmas Eve service in 1868. Ironically, even Redner said that neither he nor Brooks thought the carol or the music to it would live beyond that Christmas.

Just like the little town of Bethlehem in this endearing hymn, we never know what God can do with the little we have to offer, regardless of how small or insignificant we think it is. There's no question Phillips Brooks would have still been a famous preacher outside of the popularity of "O Little Town of Bethlehem," but it's unlikely this carol would have survived without the contributions of Lewis Redner.

O Little Town of Bethlehem

O little town of Bethlehem
How still we see thee lie
Above thy deep and dreamless sleep
The silent stars go by
Yet in thy dark streets shineth
The everlasting Light
The hopes and fears of all the years
Are met in thee tonight

For Christ is born of Mary
And gathered all above
While mortals sleep, the angels keep
Their watch of wondering love
O morning stars together
Proclaim the holy birth
And praises sing to God the King
And Peace to men on earth

How silently, how silently
The wondrous gift is given!
So God imparts to human hearts
The blessings of His heaven.
No ear may hear His coming,
But in this world of sin,
Where meek souls will receive him still,
The dear Christ enters in.

O holy Child of Bethlehem
Descend to us, we pray
Cast out our sin and enter in
Be born to us today

We hear the Christmas angels
The great glad tidings tell
O come to us, abide with us
Our Lord Emmanuel

O Little Town of Bethlehem – Brooks Version

O little town of Bethlehem,
How still we see thee lie!
Above thy deep and dreamless sleep
The silent stars go by.
Yet in thy dark streets shineth
The everlasting Light;
The hopes and fears of all the years
Are met in thee tonight.

For Christ is born of Mary,
And gathered all above,
While mortals sleep, the angels keep
Their watch of wond'ring love.
O morning stars, together
Proclaim the holy birth,
And praises sing to God the King,
And peace to men on earth!

How silently, how silently,
The wondrous Gift is giv'n;
So God imparts to human hearts
The blessings of His Heav'n.
No ear may hear His coming,
But in this world of sin,
Where meek souls will receive Him still,
The dear Christ enters in.

Where children pure and happy
Pray to the blessed Child,
Where misery cries out to Thee,
Son of the mother mild;

Where charity stands watching
And faith holds wide the door,
The dark night wakes, the glory breaks,
And Christmas comes once more.

O holy Child of Bethlehem,
Descend to us, we pray;
Cast out our sin, and enter in,
Be born in us today.
We hear the Christmas angels
The great glad tidings tell;
Oh, come to us, abide with us,
Our Lord Emmanuel!

Week 3, Day 16

O LITTLE TOWN OF BETHLEHEM

But you, O Bethlehem Ephrathah, who are too little to be among the clans of Judah, from you shall come forth for me one who is to be ruler in Israel, whose coming forth is from of old, from ancient days. Micah 5:2

H ave you ever felt small and insignificant? Like nothing you could ever do would make any difference in the grand scheme of things? And why shouldn't we when considering that we're one among eight billion people who inhabit this tiny planet in a vast, gigantic universe? Sometimes we feel insignificant when in the presence of those who appear smarter and full of self-confidence and self-importance. Still others have suffered at the hands of parents, teachers, employers, and others who have ridiculed and put them down in some way.

Nearly everyone struggles with feelings of insignificance at one time or another, regardless of who you are. Some of the greatest heroes of Scripture battled these same feelings, including David, Gideon, Ruth, Esther, and yes, even the earthly parents of Christ, but God still chose them to bring about his great purposes.

Besides penning a beloved Christmas carol, Phillips Brooks also wrote, "It is while you are patiently toiling at the little tasks of life that the meaning and shape of the great whole of life dawns on you." And so it is with the little town of Bethlehem. When Brooks visited the city, it was still a small village, slightly larger than it was at the birth of Christ and not the bustling city it would later become. Years later, as he reflected on his trip, he would write the descriptive words that would forever be enshrined in the memories of millions as they sing each year of a "little town" called Bethlehem.

In Micah, the Hebrew word translated as "little" was not so much in reference to its geographical size but rather its insignificance. The village was an unimportant little place about five miles south of Jerusalem—with one significant exception. Bethlehem was the birthplace of King David, who had received God's promise that his descendant would reign forever.

God seems to delight in upsetting human expectations, evident by the way his glory entered human life. He came as a vulnerable infant born to poor peasants in a stable in Bethlehem, not to royalty in some palace in Jerusalem. He came in the most insignificant way, to insignificant people, to an insignificant town. He did not come in power but in absolute weakness as a tiny, helpless baby.

We find the promise of Micah in the underlying message of this first line of this hymn—that no one is insignificant. It doesn't matter where you're from, how you were raised, what you've done, or how small and insignificant you think you are; God can use you. The question is not whether God uses the small, the powerless, and the vulnerable of the world. He's already proven that He does. The real question is whether you're prepared to be surprised by how he might use you to contribute to his Kingdom. Don't count yourself out. You simply need to be made available to him.

THE HOPES AND FEARS OF ALL THE YEARS

"Lord, now you are letting your servant depart in peace, according to your word; for my eyes have seen your salvation." Luke 2:29–30

D o you have a bucket list—a collection of goals, dreams, and experiences that you hope to accomplish within your lifetime? Some popular bucket list items include traveling to exotic locations, seeing a natural wonder, starting a business, writing a novel, running a marathon, learning to play an instrument, skydiving, and many more. You probably have a few of your own to add to the list.

A bucket list, though, is not a new thing. Take Simeon for instance. He was a righteous and devout man living in Jerusalem during the birth of Christ who had only one item on his bucket list: to see the Messiah before he died. This would not have been considered an unusual bucket list item for the day. In fact, most of his fellow Jews would likely check that same box, although never believing it would happen in their lifetime. Simeon, though, was unique in that he knew it would come to pass. He had a very good reason to believe such. You see, he had a guarantee from the Holy Spirit that he would not die until he had seen the Christ with his own eyes.

We can only imagine the day in which the Spirit moved Simeon to the temple at just the right moment to see Jesus there with Mary and Joseph. The insurmountable joy he felt in his heart would have been overwhelming. Everything that he and the nation of Israel had hoped for and been promised through the centuries had finally come to pass. In that moment, the Holy Spirit's promise to Simeon had been fulfilled.

Simeon recognized the gravity of the moment. Since his Holy Spirit revelation, he'd lived with no expectation of death. He had a guarantee of life—that is, until the day he saw the Messiah. Now that day had come. He could have simply turned and walked away, giving praise to God knowing he could now die in peace. But that's not what Simeon did. No, he decided to add one more item to his bucket list.

Slowly, he walked over to Mary and Joseph, wondering the whole time if he should turn back. But he couldn't. Some force was drawing him—a force that he could not describe. This was never promised to him though. What if they refused? Still, he leaned over and gently took the tiny baby from Mary's hesitant arms. He pulled the Christ child close to him, embracing the King of kings, the Redeemer, the Consolation of Israel in his arms. This was the moment he had really always wanted! Suddenly the Holy Spirit came upon him as he prophesied Jesus as the salvation of the world who would deliver truth not only to those in Israel but also to the Gentiles, all while the child's parents stood in amazement.

It's been said that the only people who fear death are those with regrets. Simeon had no regrets. For years, he waited patiently for God's promise to be fulfilled, hoping, believing, and knowing in his heart that it would. Now, as he stood gazing into the eyes of God himself, he could die in peace knowing the hopes and fears of all of humanity were delivered in the baby lying in his arms. Thus, for Simeon, the lyrics found in this hymn were true: "the hopes and fears of all the years are met in Thee tonight."

Week 3, Day 18

FOR CHRIST IS BORN OF MARY

And he came to her and said, "Greetings, O favored one, the Lord is with you!" Luke 1:28

The acronym VIP, or very important person, seems to have been coined during World War II by British officers in the Royal Air Force in charge of organizing flights for important military leaders. In order to conceal the names from enemy spies, each of these leaders were referred to as a "VIP." in the flight plan. It made sense to differentiate the senior-most officials, who were provided extra security and protection. Today we might use the term to refer to those who have been accorded special privileges because of their high social status, influence, or importance.

At first it would appear the angel Gabriel conferred God's VIP status upon Mary when referring to her as highly favored. This might seem quite odd since Mary was not one of high social status, influence, or importance. She was a poor, young, teenage girl engaged to a local carpenter who, apart from this angelic visit, would have been forgotten in the annals of history, along with most of us.

However, Mary's newly assigned favored status did not come with an easy life filled with one blessing after another, absent of trouble or worry. Instead, she was impregnated by the Holy Spirit, which called her integrity and morality into question. Had an angel not intervened, she would have been divorced from her fiancé, Joseph, and disgraced in the community, not to mention the possibility of being stoned. Surely, though, when it came time to give birth to the Son of God, she would have been afforded the best location, treatment, and hospitality. Well, nine months into her pregnancy, she and her husband had to make a difficult and dangerous trip to Bethlehem. There she would give birth to the King of kings in a cave using a feeding trough instead of a baby bed. Not exactly the VIP treatment you might come to expect with such an honor. Then, to add to her pain, many years later she would witness the horrific trauma of her son being tortured, crucified, and killed on a cross.

Those who knew Mary when she was found to be with child but not yet married probably didn't consider her blessed. Perhaps when you reflect on how God blesses you, you think about good health, your spouse, children, grandchildren, and even material things. Those can be blessings indeed.

But God never promised Mary a life absent of pain, suffering, and loss. He promised her the blessing of new life. And when she held that blessing of new life in her arms, she would never be the same. She also never could have imagined how this tiny baby would deliver that same blessing of new life, both in this world and eternity, to all those who would accept it.

Mary was highly favored not because of who she was or anything she had done. She was highly favored because God had chosen her to be the vessel to give birth to the Messiah. In John 15:16, Jesus said that you, too, have been chosen and appointed to fulfill God's work. Not all of it will feel like a blessing. In fact, there will be moments that feel like the exact opposite. God is no doubt in those moments too, but his plans have eternal Kingdom impact in ways that we cannot imagine. When you look at it from that perspective, you realize that you, too, are highly favored!

Week 3, Day 19

HOW SILENTLY, HOW SILENTLY, THAT WONDEROUS GIFT IS GIVEN

And after the wind an earthquake, but the Lord was not in the earthquake. And after the earthquake a fire, but the Lord was not in the fire. And after the fire the sound of a low whisper. 1 Kings 19:11–12

Helen Keller once said, "Everything has its wonders, even darkness and silence." We no longer live in a culture accustomed to darkness and silence. Our world is filled with a constant barrage of noise so that when the noise is completely gone, we're uncomfortable. It's almost as if there's tension in having to face the absence of the daily distractions in our lives that come in the form of sound. And because of this noise, we're likely missing out on some really great things.

For many, Christmas can be like that—noisy. There are the sounds of spirited Christmas music, rambunctious and excited kids, the clamor of fellow shoppers, and loud family gatherings, all of which can leave a ringing in your ears. But there's also mental noise that brings with it the stress of entertaining, financial issues, loneliness, or managing the loss of a loved one absent from this year's celebrations. The noise of the holidays can easily become overwhelming, and in a sense, we end up missing Christmas.

What if we approached Christmas like a child, with a sense of wonder? Wonder is described as a feeling of surprise mingled with admiration and caused by something beautiful, unexpected, unfamiliar, or inexplicable. This would all describe the birth of Christ! It's a wonder that the King of kings didn't enter this world with fanfare, fireworks, and celebrations. Nor did God announce his presence on Earth with earthquakes, fire, or wind.

In this hymn, Brooks alludes to a "wondrous gift" given silently. When you clear away all the noise, this "wonderous gift" is simple: Jesus came into the world to give us a living, breathing demonstration of what God is like...and He did so silently. Perhaps for us to truly experience the joy of Christ's birth is indeed a silent process.

Mother Teresa said, "We need to find God, and He cannot be found in noise and restlessness. God is the friend of silence." Silence might be uncomfortable, but it gives us time to turn down both the inner and outer noise of our lives and increase awareness of what matters most. Try to find your silence this Christmas and recapture the wonder, awe, and amazement of God's wonderous gift in the birth of Jesus Christ.

Week 3, Day 20

CAST OUT OUR SIN
AND ENTER IN

You will cast all our sins into the depths of the sea.
Micah 7:19

Tashlich, which literally translates to "casting off," is a ceremony performed on the afternoon of the first day of Rosh Hashanah. The practice was inspired by Micah 7:19, and Jews symbolically cast off the sins of the previous year by tossing pebbles or breadcrumbs into flowing water. During this ritual, people think of things they've done wrong in the past year and then "throw them away" into a body of flowing water, like an ocean, river, or stream, to be carried away with the current, promising improvement in the coming year.

The prophet Micah longed for the future day when the Lord would remove the sins of his people. What Micah hoped for—the utter removal of our sin—was delivered in a tiny baby who would take all our sin to the cross to be done with for good. God, in his love, made a way for our sins to be cast out by sending the one who would save his people from their sins.

We also have that same hope when asking for God's forgiveness. First John 1:9 says that when we confess our sins, God is faithful and just to forgive us. In other words, when we ask God to forgive our sins, he will literally cast them away into the sea of forgetfulness, never to be remembered again.

The symbolic tradition of the Tashlich can be a meaningful practice. The idea of God casting sins—every sinful thought, word, deed, desire, and motivation—into the sea, where they sink like stones, never to be reunited, provides comfort and freedom.

However, let's not abuse that freedom by returning to the sea in search of sins for which we've been forgiven. Holocaust survivor Corrie ten Boom, in her book, *Tramp for the Lord*, writes, "When we confess our sins, God casts them into the deepest ocean, gone forever...I believe God then places a sign out there that says No Fishing Allowed."

If you're struggling with holding on to your past sins, ask God to help you fully believe in his gift of forgiveness and new life. Consider starting the new year by allowing God to cast away all your sins, thereby entering a new life of grace and forgiveness!

Week 3, Day 21
OUR LORD EMMANUEL

Behold, the virgin shall conceive and bear a son, and they shall call his name Immanuel. Matthew 1:23

I n a recent survey commissioned by Cigna, more than half of U.S. adults (58%) considered themselves lonely. Surprisingly, young adults are twice as likely to experience feelings of loneliness as seniors (79% to 41%). Often the Christmas holidays bring on a heightened sense of loneliness and despair for several reasons: perhaps it's been a tough year; maybe there's a loved one who passed away during the year, or a family member who's normally there for the holidays is missing; still others might be overwhelmed with disappointments, suffering, or illness.

Loneliness often leads to depression, leaving you callous to the surrounding circumstances with feelings that God is not aware or, worse, that he does not care. But God knows you're lonely, and he's with you.

We can only imagine the loneliness Mary must have felt after becoming pregnant with the Messiah. She contained the biggest news the world had ever known, and she couldn't tell anyone. Who would believe her anyway? No one—not her family, friends, or fiancé. She was utterly alone. The pressure must have been overwhelming, but God was with Mary and did not leave her in that loneliness. He sent her to be with her cousin Elizabeth, who believed Mary's story and encouraged her.

What about Joseph? He had to feel alone too after learning of Mary's pregnancy and believing she had been unfaithful to him. The biggest decision of his life—to divorce her—was before him, and only he could make it. But God was also with Joseph by sending an angel to reinforce his decision to take Mary as his wife. The decision was likely met with shock and scorn from family and neighbors. But he had Mary, Mary had him, and together they both had God, who would never leave them.

The name Immanuel holds great significance. It means God is with us. Looking back on Isaiah's prophecy, the apostle Matthew saw the promise being delivered in the birth of Christ. However, one might also say that God has always been with us throughout time, even as the psalmist cried out, "Where can I go from your Spirit? Where can I flee from your presence?" (Psalm 139:7). What's different now?

The birth of Jesus was the most extraordinary event in history in that the God of the universe took on human flesh and lived among us. In other words, he was "God with us" in that he physically became one of us! No longer with us just in spirit but in human form. He came to suffer as we suffer, to be tempted as we are tempted, and to hurt as we are hurt. Jesus also experienced loneliness at the cross after being abandoned by those closest to him. But God the Father never abandoned him. He was with him the entire time.

God Immanuel is the message of Christmas—and it's truly the best news! He is with us in the present and promises that he will always be with us forever (Matthew 28:20). If this Christmas you're experiencing feelings of loneliness, remember that you are not alone. God is there, just as he was for Mary, Joseph, and

Jesus. Reach out to him with all your heart, and allow him to deliver the peace, hope, and comfort you need most.

Week 4, Day 22

"HARK! THE HERALD ANGELS SING": A HISTORY

Imagine living in a world where singing a Christmas hymn could get you arrested. In 1647 the English Parliament passed a law making the celebration of Christmas illegal. Oliver Cromwell and his fellow Puritans believed all festivities and music celebrating Christmas were irreverent for a day that was supposed to be holy. It was over twenty years later, in 1660, after Cromwell's death, when the ban was lifted and the monarchy restored. However, the damage was done, and for the next seventy-five years, new Christmas carols were scarce.

This was the world in which Charles Wesley was born, an English Methodist leader and hymn writer. Wesley was a prolific writer, having penned in his lifetime over six thousand hymns and some three thousand poems. He was the brother of John Wesley, the famous theologian and founder of Methodism, who once said that his brother's hymnal was the best theological book in existence. Wesley considered his primary purpose in the writing of his hymns and poems to be to teach the common and poor man sound biblical doctrine.

Not long after his conversion, Wesley was walking to church one Christmas morning and was inspired by the ringing sound of church bells. This inspiration led to his writing "Hark!", which he later titled "Hymn for Christmas Day" and published it in *Hymns and Sacred Poems* in 1739.

The first line of the hymn originally read, "Hark! how all the welkin rings, Glory to the King of Kings." Ironically, many of the common people that Wesley was trying to reach were likely as baffled by the word "welkin" as we are today. Even at the time, the word wasn't commonly used, especially for those outside theological circles, and it's certainly non-existent in our vocabulary today. The word "welkin" means "vault of heaven where angels dwell." So in context, Wesley would have been calling on his listeners to, "Hear how the heavens ring because of the joyful exultation of the angels."

Wesley, however, liked the way he wrote the hymn with the words he used and had no plans to change it. Generally, the Wesley brothers were not fond of others altering their works either, even if it was to make it more palatable to the culture. They said as much in the preface to the 1780 *Collection of Hymns for the Use of the People Called Methodists*. They happily approved of any reprints of their work, provided they were unaltered. However, they adamantly refused any changes to their work, and if any were made, the Wesley name was to be removed from the newer version. It wasn't their pride that was the concern but a sense of being held responsible for any bad theology that could end up being attributed to them.

Apparently George Whitefield didn't think this request applied to friends. In 1753 the famed evangelist and preacher made several changes to the hymn without consulting his good friend Charles Wesley. The most notable change was the removal of the mysterious "welkin" line, altering the opening lines to "Hark! the herald angels sing, Glory to the newborn King." He retitled the hymn to the familiar "Hark! The Herald Angels Sing" and published it in his 1754 *Collection of Hymns for Social Worship*. There is no written documentation of Wesley's opinion of

Whitefield's changes, but it's been said that his reaction was not favorable and that he never sang this version of the hymn. Over the next thirty years, the hymn underwent additional revisions, giving us in 1782, just six years prior to Wesley's death, the lyrics we still sing today.

For the first 120 years of the song's existence, the hymn was sung to various tunes that differed greatly from today. In fact, Wesley insisted it be sung to a "slow, somber, and boring" religious tune similar to that of his Easter hymn, "Christ the Lord Is Risen Today."

This all changed in 1856 when Dr. William Cummings, a youthful organist for Waltham Abbey Parish Church, just north of London, was searching for Christmas songs. He was inspired by Whitefield's revision of Wesley's hymn but felt it needed a more upbeat tempo and began his search for new music.

An accomplished and classically trained musician himself, Cummings was also an enthusiast of one of the greatest German composers of the time, Felix Mendelssohn. At sixteen, he had once been in the choir backing Mendelssohn at a concert in London and had always admired his work, including one cantata that really caught his attention.

In 1840 Mendelssohn wrote a cantata commemorating Johann Gutenberg and the invention of the printing press. Mendelssohn was a Jewish convert to Christianity and, like Wesley, not fond of his work being adapted for other purposes. In fact, it was the composer's express wish that this particular "soldier-like" composition only be used in a purely secular manner because he felt it was too spirited to be sung with "sacred words."

Cummings was either unaware of Mendelssohn's views or simply ignored it as a suggestion and married Wesley and Whitefield's text with Mendelssohn's music. In doing so, he unknowingly created one of the most joyful and recognized Christmas carols in the world, and generations have been singing it ever since.

Cummings's arrangement was reportedly printed as early as 1857, and his adaptation quickly caught on. Not being the author of the lyrics or music, his name would never receive the same prominence as that of Wesley, Whitefield, and Mendelssohn, but his contribution is nevertheless unmistakably important. Had he not joined the works of these three men, we wouldn't have one of the most beloved and popular Christmas carols ever written.

The likelihood of Wesley's carol ever becoming a mainstay in the Christmas celebration outside of the contributions of both Whitefield and Cummings seems somewhat improbable. It's more likely that it would have ended up in a stack with the thousands of other hymns that Wesley wrote that we've never heard.

Now almost three hundred years after it was first written, "Hark! The Herald Angels Sing" provides a picturesque view of the moment when a great company of heavenly hosts appeared to the least likely group of men to announce the good news of the Savior's birth. Then they praised and gave glory to God and proclaimed peace on Earth to those with whom he is pleased.

This Christmas, may you, too, with a grateful heart, join in the angels' declaration made some two thousand years ago: "Hark! the herald angels sing, Glory to the newborn king."

Hark! The Herald Angels Sing

Hark! the herald angels sing
Glory to the newborn King;
Peace on earth and mercy mild,
God and sinners reconciled:

Joyful all ye nations rise,
Join the triumph of the skies,
With the angelic host proclaim,
Christ is born in Bethlehem:
Hark! the herald angels sing
Glory to the newborn King.

Christ, by highest heaven adored,
Christ, the everlasting Lord,
Late in time behold him come,
Offspring of a virgin's womb!

Veiled in flesh the Godhead see,
Hail the incarnate Deity!
Pleased as man with men to dwell,
Jesus, our Emmanuel:
Hark! the herald angels sing
Glory to the newborn King

Hail the heaven-born Prince of Peace!
Hail the Sun of Righteousness!
Light and life to all he brings,
Risen with healing in his wings;

Mild, he lays his glory by,
Born that man no more may die,

Born to raise the sons of earth,
Born to give them second birth:
Hark! the herald angels sing
Glory to the newborn King.

Hark! – Wesley Version

Hark how all the welkin rings,
"Glory to the King of kings,
Peace on earth, and mercy mild,
God and sinners reconciled!"

Joyful, all ye nations, rise,
Join the triumph of the skies;
Universal Nature, say,
"Christ the Lord is born to-day!

"Christ, by highest heaven adored,
Christ, the everlasting Lord,
Late in time behold Him come,
Offspring of a virgin's womb.

Veil'd in flesh, the Godhead see,
Hail the Incarnate Deity!
Pleased as man with men to appear
Jesus, our Immanuel here!

Hail the heavenly Prince of Peace!
Hail the Sun of Righteousness!
Light and life to all He brings,
Risen with healing in His wings.

Mild He lays His glory by,
Born—that man no more may die,
Born—to raise the sons of earth,
Born—to give them second birth.

Come, Desire of Nations, come,

Fix in us Thy humble home;
Rise, the woman's conquering Seed,
Bruise in us the serpent's head.

Now display Thy saving power,
Ruin'd nature now restore;
Now in mystic union join
Thine to ours, and ours to Thine.

Adam's likeness, Lord, efface,
Stamp Thy image in its place;
Second Adam from above,
Reinstate us in Thy love.

Let us Thee, though lost, regain,
Thee, the Life, the Inner Man:
O to all Thyself impart,
Form'd in each believing heart

Week 4, Day 23

HARK! THE HERALD ANGELS SING

And suddenly there was with the angel a multitude of the heavenly host praising God and saying, "Glory to God in the highest, and on earth peace among those with whom he is pleased!" Luke 2:13–14

"A nd *suddenly*..." This is how some moments in life happen, don't they? *Suddenly.* Unexpected, with no warning or time to prepare. A moment in time passes, and *suddenly* your life has changed forever. These moments can be joyful, like the surprise of seeing an old friend or receiving money at a time you needed it most. But these moments can also be heartbreaking, like when we receive a phone call with devastating news or discover that we've been let go from our dream job. There are many moments in life that happen *suddenly*. That's just how it was for the shepherds the night of Jesus' birth.

Imagine that it's just a day like any other day. You grab your rod and staff and head out to the fields outside Bethlehem to begin your workday as a shepherd. It's not a glamorous job, and every day seems pretty much the same. But you join the other shepherds and spend your day protecting the flock from preying animals, guiding them to green pastures where they can eat, and finding sources of accessible drinking water. Then, at night, you bring all the sheep back into the fold, counting them as they pass and ensuring that none are missing. The days are long, but the nights are even longer as you keep watch for any wolf or thief attempting to infiltrate and snatch one of the lambs. Your livelihood depends on the safety and well-being of these sheep, and you certainly aren't going to lose one tonight.

And *suddenly*, life changes in a moment!

You're in complete awe, rendered speechless and surrounded by a heavenly host of angels all praising God! Sure, you're afraid, as anyone with blood flowing through their veins would be, but right now you're also basking in the glory of the Lord, never wanting it to end. Then, *suddenly*, it ends just as quickly as it began as the heavenly multitude returns to heaven. Once again, it's just you, your fellow shepherds, and a bunch of sheep. But something is different. It's far too difficult to describe, but *suddenly* you find yourself racing through the streets of Bethlehem, desperately trying to find a baby in a manger.

Now imagine that you're Mary or Joseph. You're in an unfamiliar town with no friends, family, or acquaintances. No one knows you, your story, or anything about this baby lying in a manger before you in the middle of the night. And *suddenly*, a group of smelly, sweaty shepherds descend on your quiet presence telling incredible stories of angels, a Savior, and a baby in swaddling clothes in a manger. No stranger to angelic visits yourself, you believe them.

These events might have been unforeseen by the shepherds and Mary and Joseph, but they were not for God. The birth of Christ was no random act or happenstance. It was a well-planned, orchestrated event that God had been slowly working out since the beginning of time.

Everyone has moments when life suddenly takes an unexpected turn, but God is not surprised by any of it. And because of our limited understanding, we may have no idea what God is doing, but we can rest in his steadfast love that surrounds us, just like the shepherds did that one magnificent night.

Week 4, Day 24

GOD AND SINNERS RECONCILED

For in him all the fullness of God was pleased to dwell, and through him to reconcile to himself all things, whether on earth or in heaven, making peace by the blood of his cross. Colossians 1:19–20

Christmas is such a special time of the year that helps bring family, friends, and loved ones together. It's a time of peace and goodwill toward your fellow neighbor. Yet for many, heartwarming thoughts of family gatherings seem elusive at best as they struggle to find peace in relationships strained by prolonged estrangement and uncertainty. During the holidays, these tense feelings escalate, making the Christmas season seem not so peaceful.

Jesus was and is a peacemaker. He is, in fact, the Prince of Peace and profoundly cares about reconciliation. It was for that reason Jesus the Son of God was born into this world to repair what was broken and to reconcile the world to himself. God is holy and righteous, and our sin separates us from him. So Jesus took the initiative. He came when we were not expecting him and had lost hope. He came humbly with no pride, only forgiveness, so that we could be reconciled to him.

The word reconcile means "to make good again," "to repair," and "to bring back to a former state of harmony." In other words, we end all hostility and restore peace. This is what Christ did by putting on the flesh of man and taking our sins upon himself, satisfying God's justice. He did what we could not do so that we could have peace with God and be reconciled to him through a relationship with Jesus Christ.

Many things can stand in the way of true reconciliation: pride, bitterness, anger, resentment, and miscommunication. Sometimes an examination of our own hearts for these feelings might help determine where we need to seek God's help.

Reconciliation is at the heart of Christmas. It's the perfect time for renewal with family and friends and inviting someone back into your life again. Jesus humbly came and showed us what love and restoration look like. Unfortunately, reconciliation is not always possible and, sometimes, not advisable. But we should never lose hope. As much as it is possible with you, settle differences quickly this Christmas. If any disagreements remain that prevent reconnecting, maybe it's time to disconnect from the anger, pain, and feelings of being wronged and to set yourself free.

Week 4, Day 25
JOYFUL ALL YE NATIONS RISE

And the angel said to them, "Fear not, for behold, I bring you good news of great joy that will be for all the people." Luke 2:10

The angelic proclamation to the shepherds that night was not for "great happiness" but for "great joy." No doubt this awe-inspiring moment provided feelings of both happiness and joy for those shepherds. But happiness did not drive them through the streets of Bethlehem that night to share with "all the people" about the Savior's birth. Joy did—a "great joy."

Often we equate joy with happiness, and there's much debate on the topic. But the idea that holds the most sway today is that happiness, by and large, depends on external factors. Even though we may want to be happy, it's not a choice we make but rather the byproduct of some external factor or event that activates one of our senses and is largely dependent on circumstances.

For example, psychologists have confirmed that Christmas decorating can spike dopamine, a feel-good hormone that creates a neurological shift in our minds, producing feelings of happiness. The same can be said for family gatherings, gift giving, and your favorite holiday treat. It's an event that triggers nostalgic feelings of days gone by that we register in our happiness bucket.

Joy, on the other hand, is a choice purposefully made. Joy embraces inner feelings of peace and contentment regardless of circumstances. We might not be happy in the moment, as in times of grief and uncertainty, but we can still feel joy. And in choosing joy, we find hope that sustains us in the most difficult of times.

How, then, like the shepherds, do we embrace the spirit of "greater joy" this Christmas? Psalm 16:11 says that in the Lord's presence, there is fullness of joy. The simple truth is that joy is found by spending time with God and thanking him for the "good news that is for everyone." This news is meant to be shared, and that's just what the shepherds did by becoming the first evangelists with a birth announcement.

Perhaps if you're searching for a "greater joy" this Christmas, you can look to the example of the shepherds as you share the good news that is meant for "all the people" with all the people you know. There can be no greater joy!

Week 4, Day 26
VEILED IN FLESH, THE GODHEAD SEE

And the Word became flesh and dwelt among us, and we have seen his glory, glory as of the only Son from the Father, full of grace and truth. John 1:14

"Hark! The Herald Angels Sing" consistently ranks as one of the top Christmas carols of all time. It's filled with rich imagery and theological truth surrounding the birth of Christ. But we must wonder as the carol rings out in churches all over the world on Christmas Eve how many of us, without thinking what we're saying—believers and unbelievers alike—repeat over and over the most important concept of Christian theology: that of a deity being embodied in human flesh.

The apostle John took his own unique perspective on the nativity, which is somewhat different from what you'll find in the gospels of Matthew and Luke. In his own captivating style, John looks deeper into the manger and sees the Creator of the world, who has existed from all eternity, stepping into the world as Jesus Christ and becoming the visible expression of the invisible God.

When Jesus was physically born a man, he never stopped being God. His deity was hidden or veiled in his flesh. Otherwise, he would have walked around in the glory of the Lord, and in our sin, we could not have stood before him. Jesus was the Incarnate Deity. He was God expressing himself in a way that we could relate to him and understand. This is the mystery of the Incarnation that John is describing: that God would lay aside his glory for the souls of men and women and then announce to the world that he is here.

When Jesus stepped into our world, He came bearing two gifts: grace and truth. Grace is God's unmerited favor. It is kindness from God that we don't deserve. Truth, on the other hand, is that which is consistent with the mind, will, character, glory, and being of God. It demands justice, and justice demands punishment for wrongdoing. Grace and truth must work in tandem. Grace without truth is easily seen as sentimentality, while truth without grace breeds self-righteousness and legalism.

The truth is that in his fullness of grace, he was able to pay for our sins and offer us a complete pardon—one that we did not deserve. This is indeed good news! Perhaps the one present the world needs, or maybe you need, this Christmas is the gift of grace and truth.

When you hear or sing this carol this year, pay close attention to the deep, rich meaning behind the words. Be in awe of the Incarnation and how great God's love is for you!

LIGHT AND LIFE TO ALL HE BRINGS

Again Jesus spoke to them, saying, "I am the light of the world. Whoever follows me will not walk in darkness, but will have the light of life." John 8:12

F or centuries, lighthouses have been beacons of hope for seafarers. Ida Lewis was just twelve years old when her father suffered a stroke, and she became the lighthouse keeper on the tiny island of Lime Rock off the coast of Rhode Island. Each day, she climbed the tower and filled the lamp with oil at dusk. At midnight, she trimmed the wick and polished carbon off reflectors, and she put out the light at dawn. In the fall of 1854, when she was twelve, she saw four young men capsize their sailboat. She rowed out to rescue them and pulled them into her rowboat. That was the first of many rescues. Over the space of forty-six years, Ida Lewis faithfully kept the lamp lit at Lime Rock Light Station and rescued as many as thirty-six people from drowning.

Trusting God is much like trusting the beckoning light of the lighthouse. You row toward the light, trusting that your life will be saved amid the darkness of the storm.

In the darkness of creation, God commanded there be light. Then, once again, he commanded there be light two thousand years ago in Bethlehem. In doing so, he pushed back the spiritual darkness that had permeated the world with a light so bright that darkness had to flee.

Just as a lighthouse illuminates waterways, guiding mariners along perilous, rocky coasts, Jesus truly is the Light of the World, illuminating the truth about God and life. His light guides us, scattering the darkness as it points the way and keeping watch over us as we wait for dawn to come.

The celebration of Advent highlights the interplay between light and darkness and the coming of Jesus as the light of the world. Each week, we light another candle on the Advent wreath, watching it grow brighter and brighter until, finally, on Christmas Day (or Christmas Eve) we light the Christ candle signifying that the Light of the World has been born!

This is why Christ came: to bring light into our darkness and to bring us freedom and new life. On that first Christmas, light pierced the darkness, and the darkness has not overcome it. It continues to shine for all to see. We no longer need to stumble around in spiritual darkness; we have the light of Christ by which we walk. Whatever we're facing in life, Jesus came to bring light to that situation. Choose to follow the Light of the World and then, like Ida Lewis, become the lightkeeper and fan his light bright for others to see.

BORN TO GIVE THEM SECOND BIRTH

Jesus said to her, "I am the resurrection and the life. Whoever believes in me, though he die, yet shall he live, and everyone who lives and believes in me shall never die. Do you believe this?" John 11:25–26

Martha was grief-stricken. Her brother, Lazarus, had just succumbed to an illness and died. Several days earlier, she had sent word to the Master informing him of the grave situation of one of his dearest friends. Now it was too late. In her heart, she knew that had Jesus come when requested, her brother would still be alive. Questions flooded her mind: Where was he? Why was he waiting so long to come? Why was he there for so many others but not her brother?

Hearing that the teacher had arrived in the village, Martha hurried out to meet him and could not restrain her grief and disappointment, crying out, "Lord, if you had been here, my brother would not have died." Still, somehow, just being in his presence soothed her as he affectionately proclaimed that Lazarus would rise again. Martha believed her brother would rise from the grave someday...in the last day. She didn't doubt that at all. But that was in the future. What about today? She needed comfort right now.

Jesus could have immediately gone to the grave and raised Lazarus. But that's not what he did. No one was expecting him to anyway, believing all was lost. So instead, he took the opportunity to teach Martha about himself—that he is the resurrection and the life and those who believe in him will ultimately not die at all. Then, gently peering into Martha's broken heart, he asked her a significant question: "Do you believe this?"

Martha might not have realized it at the moment, but her faith in Jesus was much too small in her mind and heart. She had limited him to what she thought he should or could do. Jesus, however, was trying to stretch Martha's faith beyond a belief that her brother would be raised in the last day. "Think bigger, Martha!" you can almost hear Jesus say. "When you believe in me, your true self will never die! Your life is now fused with mine. Do you believe this?"

This is the question of faith. It's a simple question with eternal significance, and it's a question Jesus continues to ask to all those who encounter him. And more people encounter him during Christmas than any other time of the year. As you prepare your own heart for the coming of the Lord this Christmas, pray for those you know who, like Martha, are hurting and wondering when Jesus will show up. They, like each of us, are presented with the same question: "Do you believe this?" I sincerely hope that you do. If you do, then nothing will ever be the same again.

God bless and merry Christmas!

Leave a Review

Thank you again for reading this book! I hope and pray that in some way it encouraged you (and your group) to grow closer to Christ.

If you enjoyed this book, I would appreciate your leaving an honest review for the book and study on Amazon! Your review will help others know if this devotional is right for them.

It's easy and will only take a minute. Just search for "The Carols of Christmas, Alan Vermilye" on Amazon. Click on the product in the search results, and then click on reviews.

I would also love to hear from you! Drop me a note by visiting me at www.BrownChairBooks.com and clicking on "Contact."

Thank you and God bless!

Alan

Free Devotional

The Proverbs Devotional Challenge

31 Daily Devotions to Deepen Your Knowledge, Wisdom, and Understanding

Studies reveal that a mere 9% of people who make New Year's resolutions actually follow through. Rather than making a typical resolution this year, challenge yourself to read one chapter in Proverbs every day in January. It's perfect because there are 31 chapters and 31 days in January!

The Book of Proverbs is a great source of wisdom on how to live your life according to God's desires and to gain knowledge and understanding. This book of the Bible covers topics such as life, family, parenting, friendships, work, finances, heart matters, and the power of our words.

In addition, I've created 31 devotions, one for each day, to help you explore valuable insights and apply them to your life. It's free to download, and you can get it either directly to your e-reader or as a PDF.

If you want to grow spiritually, intellectually, and emotionally, this challenge is ideal for you. The Proverbs Devotional Challenge is a great way to deepen your faith, no matter where you are on your journey.

Get Your Free Devotional Today!

www.BrownChairBooks.com/FreeDevo

The Carols of Christmas Volume 2

Daily Advent Devotions on Classic Christmas Carols
By Alan Vermilye

The Carols of Christmas Volume 2 is a collection of devotionals based on beloved carols that will inspire readers to reflect on the true meaning of Christmas. In this 28-day devotional journey, you will experience a fresh take on familiar melodies with personal reflections to guide you.

The carols include "Silent Night", "Joy to the World", "O Come All Ye Faithful", and "The First Noel". You'll also discover intriguing stories and thought-provoking details like who wrote the carol; what was going on in their life that perhaps inspired the hymn; and how has God used this hymn throughout time:

The book is divided into four weeks of daily devotions, perfect for celebrating Advent or Christmas. Each week you begin by reading the history of the carol, followed by six daily devotions that reflect on a verse from the hymn along with a Scripture reflection. Traditionally, Advent begins on the fourth Sunday before Christmas, but the devotions are undated, allowing you to start any time.

www.BrownChairBooks.com

A Christmas Carol Study Guide

Book and Bible Study Based on A Christmas Carol

By Alan Vermilye

A Christmas Carol Book and Bible Study Guide includes the entire book of this Dickens classic as well as Bible study discussion questions for each chapter, Scripture references, and related commentary.

Detailed character sketches and an easy-to-read book summary provide deep insights into each character while examining the book's themes of greed, isolation, guilt, blame, compassion, generosity, transformation, forgiveness, and, finally, redemption. To help with those more difficult discussion questions, a complete answer guide is available for free online.

What others are saying:

"The study is perfect for this time of the year, turning our focus to the reason for the season—Jesus—and the gift of redemption we have through him." – Connie

"I used this for an adult Sunday School class. We all loved it!" – John

"This study is wonderful!" – Lori

"I found this a refreshing look at the Bible through the eyes of Ebenezer Scrooge's life." – Lynelle

It's a Wonderful Life Study Guide

A Bible Study Based on the Christmas Classic It's a Wonderful Life

By Alan Vermilye

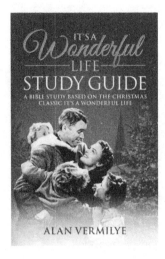

It's a Wonderful Life is one of the most popular and heart-warming films ever made. It's near-universal appeal and association with Christmas has provided a rich story of redemption that has inspired generations for decades.

It's a Wonderful Life Study Guide examines this beloved holiday classic and reminds us how easily we can become distracted from what is truly meaningful in life. This five-week Bible study experience comes complete with discussion questions for each session, Scripture references, detailed character sketches, movie summary, and related commentary. In addition, a complete answer guide and video segments for each session are available for free online.

What others are saying:

"Thank you, Alan, for the unforgettable experience. Your book has prompted me to see and learn much more than merely enjoying the film, It's a Wonderful Life." – Er Jwee

"The questions got us all thinking, and the answers provided were insightful and encouraging. I would definitely encourage Home Groups to study this!" – Jill

"It's a Wonderful Life Study Guide by Alan Vermilye is intelligent, innovative, interesting, involving, insightful, and inspirational." – Paul

www.BrownChairBooks.com

The Pilgrim's Progress

A Readable Modern-Day Version of John Bunyan's Pilgrim's Progress

By Alan Vermilye

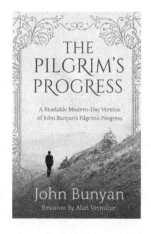

Reading The Pilgrim's Progress by John Bunyan can be a bit challenging even for the best of readers. Not so with this new, easy-to-read version that translates the original archaic language into simple conversational English allowing readers of all ages to easily navigate the most popular Christian allegory of all time.

Without losing any faithfulness to the original text, now you can read Bunyan's timeless classic and reimagine this famous quest that has challenged and encouraged believers for centuries.

What others are saying:

"Phenomenal! Finally able to read The Pilgrims Progress!!!" – Sandra

"What a blessing! Definitely one of the ten books that I have ever read." – TC

"Wow!! This book lights a fire in your heart for sure. Thank you Alan for an accurate revision so that i may understand." – Jesse

"Try reading this book, if you dare. You will find you identify with more than one characters in the book." – Jon

The Pilgrim's Progress Study Guide

A Bible Study Based on John Bunyan's Pilgrim's Progress

By Alan Vermilye

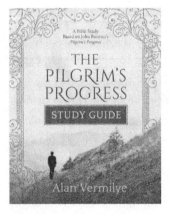

Understanding The Pilgrim's Progress by John Bunyan can be difficult and confusing at times. Not so with The Pilgrim's Progress Study Guide! This comprehensive Bible study workbook will guide you through Bunyan's masterful use of metaphors helping you better understand key concepts, supporting Bible passages, and the relevance to our world today.

Designed to be used alongside The Pilgrim's Progress: A Readable Modern-Day Version of John Bunyan's Pilgrim's Progress, each chapter, sub section, and study question examines Bunyan's allegorical narrative to tell his powerful presentation of what it means to follow the narrow way of Christian salvation.

What others are saying:

"This was a tour de force trip through scripture with rich discussions each week. I highly recommend it!" – Stan

"Invaluable book! My wife and I started rereading The Pilgrims Progress, so I got thi study guide, so happy I did! Great study questions yo make you think." – Mark

"I heartily recommend the combination of Pilgrim's Progress and Pilgrim's Progress Study Guide by Alan Vermilye. You'll be glad you took the time to do this study." – Paul

www.BrownChairBooks.com

The Screwtape Letters Study Guide

A Bible Study on the C.S. Lewis Book The Screwtape Letters

By Alan Vermilye

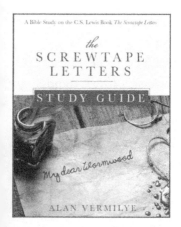

The Screwtape Letters Study Guide takes participants through a study of C.S. Lewis's classic, The Screwtape Letters. This Bible study digs deep into each letter from Screwtape, an undersecretary in the lowerarchy of Hell, to his incompetent nephew Wormwood, a junior devil.

Perfect for small group sessions, this interactive workbook includes daily, individual study with a complete answer guide available online. Designed as a 12-week study, multiple-week format options are also included.

What others are saying:

"This book and study creates a positive reinforcement on fighting that spiritual battle in life. Great read, great study guide!" – Lester

"This study guide was a wonderful way for our group to work through The Screwtape Letters!" – Becky

"Use this study guide for a fresh 'seeing' of The Screwtape Letters!" – William

www.BrownChairBooks.com

Mere Christianity Study Guide

A Bible Study on the C.S. Lewis Book Mere Christianity

By Steven Urban

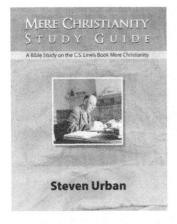

Mere Christianity Study Guide takes participants through a study of C. S. Lewis classic Mere Christianity. Yet despite its recognition as a "classic," there is surprisingly little available today in terms of a serious study course.

This 12-week Bible study digs deep into each chapter and, in turn, into Lewis's thoughts. Perfect for small group sessions, this interactive workbook includes daily, individual study as well as a complete appendix and commentary to supplement and further clarify certain topics. Multiple week format options are also included.

What others are saying:

"This study guide is more than just a guide to C.S Lewis' Mere Christianity; it is a guide to Christianity itself." – Crystal

"Wow! What a lot of insight and food for thought! Perfect supplement to Mere Christianity. I think Mr. Lewis himself would approve." – Laurie

"Our group is in the middle of studying Mere Christianity, and I have found this guide to be invaluable." - Angela

The Problem of Pain Study Guide

A Bible Study on the C.S. Lewis Book The Problem of Pain

By Alan Vermilye

In his book, The Problem of Pain, C.S. Lewis's philosophical approach to why we experience pain can be confusing at times. The Problem of Pain Study Guide breaks down each chapter into easy-to-understand questions and commentary to help you find meaning and hope amid the pain.

The Problem of Pain Study Guide expands upon Lewis's elegant and thoughtful work, where he seeks to understand how a loving, good, and powerful God can possibly coexist with the pain and suffering that is so pervasive in the world and in our lives. As Christ-followers we might expect the world to be just, fair, and less painful, but it is not. This is the problem of pain.

What others are saying:

"Many thanks for lending me a helping hand with one of the greatest thinkers of all time!" – Adrienne

"The questions posed range from very straightforward (to help the reader grasp main concepts) to more probing (to facilitate personal application), while perhaps the greatest benefit they supply is their tie-in of coordinating scriptures that may not always be apparent to the reader." – Sphinn

www.BrownChairBooks.com

The Practice of the Presence of God

A 40-Day Devotion Based on Brother Lawrence's
The Practice of the Presence of God

By Alan Vermilye

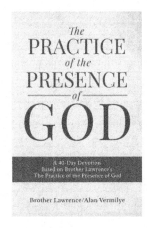

Since it was first published in 1691, The Practice of the Presence of God contains a collection of notes, letters, and interviews given by Brother Lawrence to his friends as a way of helping them turn ordinary daily life events into conversations with God.

Based on this timeless classic, The Practice of the Presence of God: A 40-Day Devotion guides readers on a 40-day journey through the wisdom of Brother Lawrence, related Scripture passages, and devotional thoughts that bring you into a more conversational relationship with God.

What others are saying:

"I love this devotional. It is short and to the point, and thus making it easy to stick to every day!" – Kathleen

"Enlightening new depths in prayer." – Kathy

"This devotional opens the door to Brother Lawrence that brings his letters and conversations to life every day!" – Steve

www.BrownChairBooks.com

Made in the USA
Monee, IL
20 November 2024

70666406R00066